PHENOMENAL!
The SMALL
book OF BIG WORDS!

PHENOMENAL!

The SMALL book OF BIG WORDS!

By Jonathan Meres

SKEDADDLE

INTREPID

BLAH BLAH BLAH BLAH BLAH BLAH

LOQUACIOUS

DOGMATIC

APOPLECTIC

First published 2011 by Macmillan Children's Books
a division of Macmillan Publishers Limited
20 New Wharf Road, London N1 9RR
Basingstoke and Oxford
Associated companies throughout the world
www.panmacmillan.com

ISBN 978-0-230-75193-4

A CIP catalogue record for this book is available from
the British Library.

Design and illustrations by New Future Graphic
Printed and bound in Great Britain by CPI Mackays, Chatham ME5 8TD

To my father,
Zbigniew Meres –
who speaks better English
than I ever did

GRANDAD FART

HOW TO USE THIS BOOK

and stuff

Using this book couldn't be easier. All you have to do is turn to the first page and read it. Once you've done that, turn the page over and read the next one. And so on and so on until you've finished – or it's teatime, or it's time to flush. If you can't be bothered reading all of it, just flick through and read random bits instead. It's up to you. You're not going to be tested! You don't even need to read this bit if you don't want to. In fact there are probably quite a few of you who *aren't* reading this bit and who by now are chuckling away because you've just come across the word *fart*, or a reference to some other bodily function. The word *fart* crops up on a fairly regular basis. Mainly, it has to be said, to annoy grown-ups. But also because it's funny and probably not what you were expecting.

You were probably expecting a bunch of words with 18 syllables that mean *a rare kind of skin infection found mainly on a badger's backside* or something, weren't you? But *big* words aren't necessarily *long* words. Some of these words are actually quite *short* words. You've probably heard quite a few of them already. That's because these are words that you can actually *use*.

Let's face it – there are only so many times you're ever going to need to know what the word for *a rare kind of skin infection found mainly on a badger's backside* is. Talking of badgers' backsides, if it *is* time to flush, please remember to wash your hands afterwards. Right, that's about it. Carry on.

1 Discover loads of big words and what they mean.

2 Learn how to drop them into everyday conversations and make yourself sound dead clever.

3 Impress relations at boring parties and stop them banging on about how kids spend their whole lives on computers and stuff.

4 Discombobulate asinine adversaries with your verbal guile.

5 Work out what the heck that last sentence meant.

6 Find out what the Lithuanian for 'malevolent' is.

7 Become fabulously popular and successful or your money back. *

* Terms and conditions apply.

ABASHED

Pronounced –
uh-bashed

Means ~
embarrassed,
uncomfortable.

As in ~
He was abashed
to find himself
naked in the middle
of assembly, but
euphoric* to discover
that it was all just a
dream.

A bit like ~
ashamed, mortified.

And ~
I'm abashed when
my mum complains
that there's no
toilet paper in the
restaurant.**

**Nothing to
do with ~**
being bashed.***

The opposite of ~
unabashed.

**If you like this
word, try ~**
abated.

---

* *Thrilled, ecstatic.*
**Toilet paper in the *toilets* – not the actual restaurant.
Battered.*
****Battered *as in *hit* – not as in *fish.*

fart cloud

abba-ray-shun

Means ~
a departure from
what is considered
normal or acceptable.

As in ~
In a moment of
aberration Grandpa
got up from the table
and set fire to a fart.*

And ~
Tidying his room
the first time he was
asked was a one-off
aberration.

A bit like ~
deviation, anomaly.

Nothing like ~
an Abba tribute
act.**

**Don't confuse
with ~**
Aberystwyth.***

---

*One of his *own* farts – not someone else's.****
**Swedish pop group. Big in the 1970s. Ask your gran.
***A small town in Wales.
****Don't try this at home kids*****
*****Wait till you're out.******
******I'm kidding. Don't try it *anywhere*. Trust me!

Means ~ to dislike something very strongly.

As in ~ I abhor it when I'm banned from the Xbox for no reason whatsoever.

And ~ Of all the soups that she abhorred she abhorred cream of sprout the most.

A bit like ~ detest, loathe.

In Dutch ~ *verafschuwen*.

Don't confuse with ~ a boar,* or a bore.**

'Nature abhors a vacuum'
– François Rabelais***

'I abhor vacuuming'
– Jonathan Meres****

---

*Male pig.
**Someone who's boring.
***Brainy French bloke.
****The not particularly brainy bloke writing this book.

APOPLECTIC

a-pop-lek-tick

Means ~
furious, enraged.

As in ~
Dad was apoplectic when he discovered he'd been given a parking ticket.

And ~
He would have been *even more* apoplectic had he known mum had just got a job as a traffic warden.

A bit like ~
seething, incandescent.

Nothing like ~
an electric popcorn maker.

Don't confuse with ~
apocalyptic.*

*Disastrous, calamitous.**
**But it wouldn't be the end of the world if you did.

ASININE

ass-a-nine

Means ~
stupid and ass-like.*

As in ~ It was asinine
of the politician to
call the interviewer a
smelly poo-head.

And ~ My teacher
was annoyed
when I called her
question asinine, but
impressed by my well
good vocabulary.

A bit like ~
fatuous, moronic.

Nothing like ~
the word after
asin*eight* and
the word before
asin*ten*.**

**If you like this
word, try ~**

assiduous

---

*That's ass as in *donkey*, by the way, in case you were wondering!***
**There are no such words. I was being *asinine*.
***Or even if you weren't.

11

BREVITY

brev-ity

BRIEFNESS

Means ~ briefness, use of few words.

As in ~ The only good thing about the trip to the lawn-mower museum was its brevity.

I SEE.

And ~ I intended making this sentence short and snappy in order to illustrate the meaning of brevity but, well, one thing led to another and the next thing I knew it was long-winded and unnecessarily complicated.

A bit like ~ succinctness, pithiness.

PITHINESS. YOU KNOW, LIKE AN ORANGE?

Nothing to do with ~ being brave.

The opposite of ~ rambling.*

In Latvian ~ *nepietiekamība***

Don't confuse with ~ levity.***

'**Those who make the worst use of their time are the first to complain of its brevity**' – Jean de la Bruyère****

---

* That's *rambling* as in *long-windedness*, not walking up hills.
** Not exactly the briefest of words for a word that's supposed to mean briefness!
*** Light-heartedness, frivolity.
**** Rhymes with Gruyère. *****
***** See *Forage*.

KEEP IT SHORT.

BR⚽UHAHA

broo-ḥa-ha

Settle down, settle down

UPROAR   WHAT!

Means ~ outcry, uproar.

As in ~ The famous footballer sparks a massive brouhaha by admitting that he frequently dives in order to get penalties.

I ♥ DIVES (+CA$H)

LOADSA MONEY!!

DIVE!!

(CROWD.)

And ~ There was an almighty brouhaha when Mr Peters walked into the class wearing a dress.

A bit like ~ hubbub, kerfuffle.

From ~ the old French word *boohoohaha*, meaning *not sure whether to laugh or cry.**

In Portuguese ~ *bafafá*.

If you like this word, try ~ palaver.

*Not really – but it *is* an old French word.

Rhymes with ~ scrumptious.

Means ~ arrogant, pushy.

As in ~ My bumptious baby brother bawls and burps all through dinner but somehow it's *me* who gets told to leave the table!

And ~ Everyone laughs as the bumptious film star trips and falls after collecting his award.*

A bit like ~ brash, swaggering.

The opposite of ~ modest, humble.

In Bulgarian ~ *самоуверен*.

Don't confuse with ~ sumptuous.**

---

* No film stars were hurt during the writing of this book. ***
** Luxurious, lavish.
*** We used a stuntman.

CAHOOTS

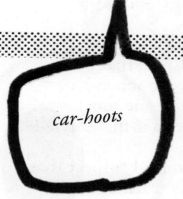

car-hoots

SNIFF

Means ~ to have a secret arrangement or agreement with somebody.*

As in ~ My teachers suspect that I am in cahoots with someone much cleverer than myself.

And ~ I suspect that my teachers are in cahoots with cheese-sniffing aliens from Planet Brie.

A bit like ~ collaborating with someone.

Nothing like ~ the honking sound that a car makes.

From ~ the French *cahute*, which means *hut* or *shed* – though quite what that's got to do with having an arrangement with someone is anybody's guess!**

If you like this word, try ~ cohort

---

*In the well-known nursery rhyme 'Hey Diddle Diddle', for instance, the dish and the spoon are clearly in *cahoots* with each other.
**Unless you've arranged to meet them in a shed.

CIRCUMVENT

sir-kum-vent

DOG DRESSED AS LION

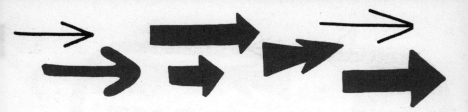

Means ~ to go around something, to outwit.

As in ~ The wily* wildebeest circumvents the lion by catching a bus.**

And ~ I circumvent having to tidy my room by paying my sister to do it instead.

A bit like ~ dodge, evade.

From ~ the Latin *circumvenine*.

First known use ~ 1539.***

If you like this word, try ~ circumspect.

*Crafty.
**Clearly a ridiculous example. Where would it keep its bus pass?
***Just after half past three.

CONDONE

cond-own

Means ~ to forgive or excuse something that's normally considered wrong or immoral.

A bit like ~ tolerate, or overlook.

The opposite of ~ condemn.

As in ~ It's possible to condone Robin Hood's actions.*

And ~ I couldn't condone putting fart powder into Dad's tea, but it *was* quite funny.**

MEGA FART TRUMPING POWDER!!

FAR-TEA! SAY IT OUT LOUD!!

STINK

---

*The stealing from the rich and giving to the poor bit – not the killing people with bows and arrows bit.
**If you weren't sitting next to Dad.

ROBIN HOOD'S HAT

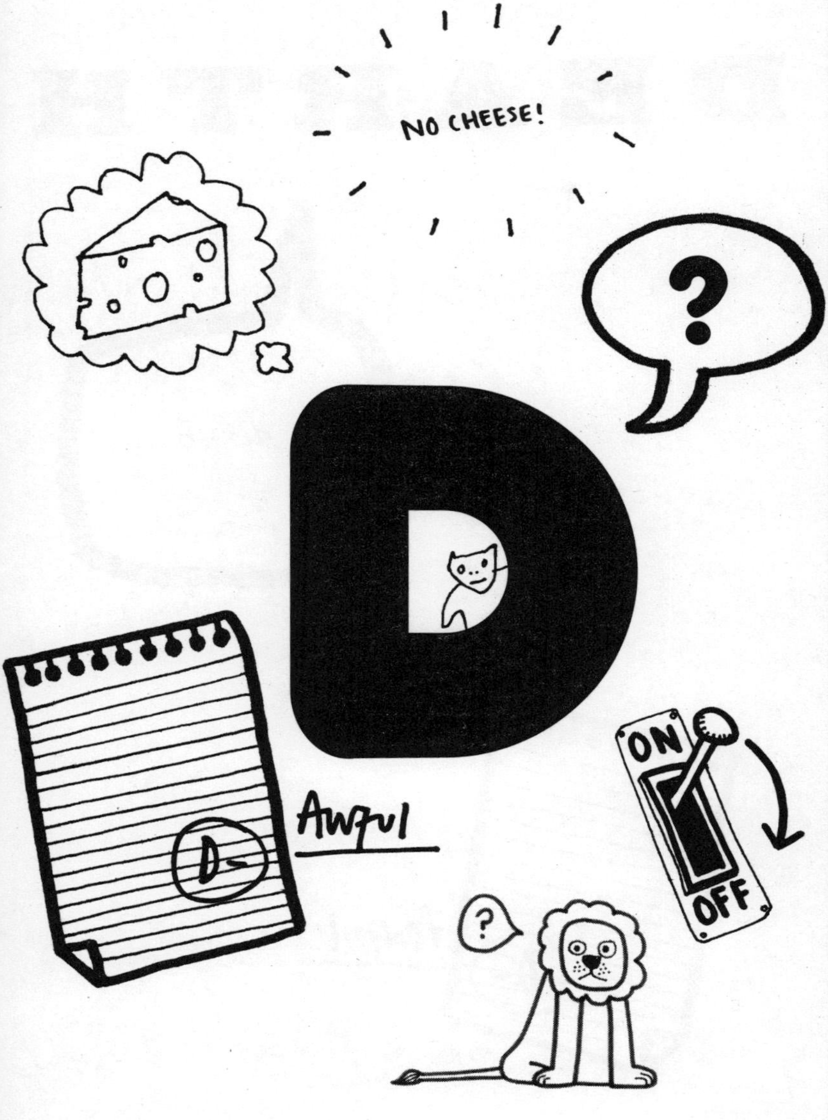
NO CHEESE!
?
D
D-
AWFUL
ON
OFF
?

DEARTH

der-th

Rhymes with ~ firth.*

Means ~ A shortage, or lack of something.

As in ~ There's a distinct dearth of cheese in the fridge.

And ~ Sadly, my homework contains a dearth of correct answers.

A bit like ~ scarcity, or deficiency.

PLENTY OF OTHER THINGS... but

NO CHEESE!

The opposite of ~ glut, or plethora.**

Don't confuse with ~ Darth.***

---

*Scottish term for river estuary – as in Firth of Forth.
**See *Plethora*.
Vader – as in 'May the *Forth* be with you.'*
****Coincidence?*****
*****No – just an excuse for a really bad joke.

DEMUR

dee-mur

Means ~
to protest, object.

As in ~ When told
by the ref that he was
marginally offside
the footballer politely
demurs.

And ~ I demur at my
dad's suggestion that
I switch off the Xbox
and begin my
homework.

A bit like ~
dispute, dissent.

The opposite of ~
agree.

**Don't confuse
with ~** demure.*
Or lemur.**

EVIL HOMEWORK

*Modest, reserved.
Small furry creature found in the rainforests of Madagascar.*
Don't confuse *lemur* with *Lima*.*
****Capital of Peru.

DISCOMBOBULATED

*dis-com-bob
-u-lated*

Means ~ thrown into confusion.

As in ~ The lion is discombobulated by the skateboarding wildebeest.

And ~ My parents are discombobulated when I suddenly start speaking Swedish.*

Don't confuse with ~ anything.

If you like this word, try ~ nincompoop.

A bit like ~ befuddled, bamboozled.

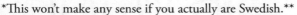

*This won't make any sense if you actually are Swedish.**
Jag är ledsen.*
Means 'I am sorry' in Swedish.*
****I don't mean I'm sorry you're Swedish – I mean I'm sorry that it won't make any sense.

DOGMATIC

dog-mat-ik

Is this something
to do with me?
Should I be here?
Woof?

Means ~ expressing strong beliefs about something without always being able to prove it.

As in ~
The dogmatic scientist claims to have discovered an eighth day of the week.

And ~ I'm not dogmatic, I'm just always right!

A bit like ~ assertive, opinionated.

Nothing like ~ some kind of futuristic robot-dog.

The opposite of ~ open-minded, flexible.

An anagram of ~ magic dot.*

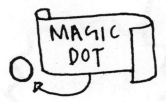

If you like this word, try ~ didactic.

---

* Pretty spooky, huh?**
** No, you're right – it's not spooky at all.

EBULLIENT

ee-bully-ent

Means ~ full of enthusiasm.

As in ~ The children skip out of school in ebullient mood and full of beans.*

From ~ the Latin *ebullire*, meaning *to bubble and boil.****

In German ~ *überschwänglich.*

And ~
My sister wasn't quite so ebullient when she found out her hamster had just been sucked up by the vacuum cleaner.**

is that a hamster?

EEK!

THAT'S A FAT HAMSTER!

A bit like ~ exuberant, buoyant.

---

*Not *literally* full of beans. That could cause quite a stink!
**No hamsters were vacuumed during the writing of this book.
***Wait a minute. Bubbling and boiling kids full of beans?
Let's skedaddle!****
****See *Skedaddle*.

ENAMOURED

en-am-urd

Means ~ charmed, captivated by something or someone.

As in ~ I was enamoured with her the moment I heard her burp the alphabet.

A bit like ~ smitten, infatuated.

Nothing to do with ~ putting on armour.

From ~ the French *en amour*, literally 'in love'.

'Mine ear is much enamoured of thy note' – William Shakespeare, *A Midsummer Night's Dream*.

And ~ He was less than enamoured with the smell of the Camembert.*

---

*Popular French cheese which if left too long can end up smelling like a sumo wrestler's jockstrap.**
**Apparently, anyway. I've never actually smelt one.

EPHEMERAL

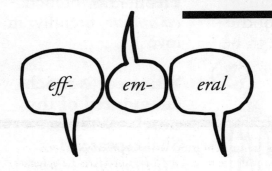

eff- *em-* *eral*

Means ~ short-lived, momentary.

As in ~ Luckily the trend for see-through trousers in the 1980s was only ephemeral.*

And ~ Her good mood proved to be as ephemeral as a lamb's fart.**

A bit like ~ fleeting, leaving no trace.

The opposite of ~ lasting, enduring.

An anagram of ~ elepheram.***

*Luckily the trend for transparent pants was even *more* ephemeral.
**There's no scientific evidence to suggest that lamb's farts are ephemeral, but I like to think they are.
***Cross between an elephant and a sheep.

ees-shoo

Means ~ to avoid, or have nothing to do with something.

As in ~ It's best to eschew Grandpa's company when he's been eating cheese.

A bit like ~ shun, abstain from.

Nothing to do with ~ the sound you make when you sneeze.

Don't confuse with ~ Escheweg.*

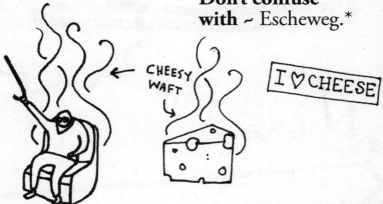

CHEESY WAFT

I ♡ CHEESE

And ~ I eschew the tidying of my room and watch TV instead.

*A street in Eschen, one of the largest municipalities in Liechtenstein.**
One of the smallest countries in the world.*
The world's largest producer of false teeth.*
*****True or false?******
******True.

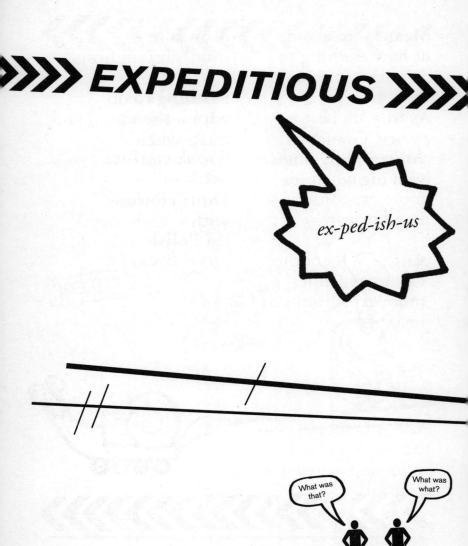

Means ~
speedy, efficient.

As in ~ Why bother
walking when it's
more expeditious
to go by car?*

And ~ Why bother
talking when it's
more expeditious to
text?

A bit like ~
rapid, prompt.

**Don't confuse
with ~**
expialidocious**

In Polish ~
spożytkowaniu.

*Calm down! I'm joking!***
**As in *supercalifragilistic.*
***I do my bit for the environment. I've been recycling the same jokes for
years.

FASTIDIOUS

fas-tiddy-us

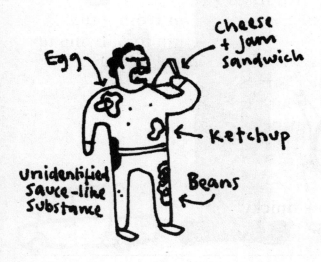

Egg

cheese
+ jam
sandwich

Ketchup

unidentified
sauce-like
substance

Beans

fig.1 NOT fastidious.

Means ~ incredibly fussy.

As in ~ The coach was fastidious in his pre-match preparation and knew not only the star sign of each opposing player, but their mother's maiden name and what their favourite colour was.*

And ~ It's a pity my little brother isn't as fastidious about his personal hygiene as he is about what he eats.

A bit like ~ finicky, pernickety.

The opposite of ~ indifferent, easy-going.

Not from ~ the Latin for 'tidying up really quickly'.

---

*The *player's* favourite colour – not their *mother's*.**
**That would be a bit *too* fastidious!

FEASIBLE

feez-ib-ul

Rhymes with ~ squeezable.

Means ~ possible, realistic.

As in ~ It's feasible that one day humans could live on the Moon.*

And ~ Living on a planet ruled by cheese-eating badgers is not feasible.**

A bit like ~ plausible, viable.

Don't confuse with ~ freezable.***

---

*But only once they've built an IKEA there.*****
**See *Forage*.
Confusing *feasible* and *freezable* could lead to all kinds of hilarious misunderstandings!*
****Unfortunately I can't think of any at the moment.
*****Other retail outlets selling flat-pack wardrobes and little candles are available.

FECKLESS

fek-less

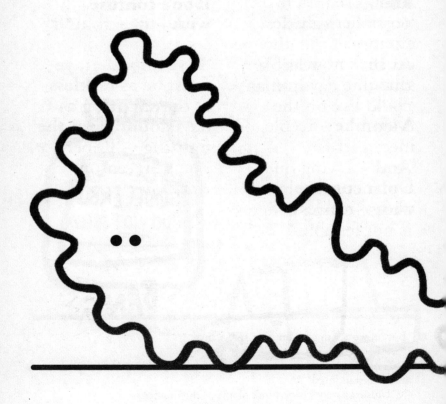

Means ~ good for nothing, useless.

As in ~ She watches her feckless father fail to fix the family car.

And ~ Thanks to her father's feckless attempts to fix the car she's now late for school.

A bit like ~ feeble, incompetent.

Don't confuse with – reckless.*

In German ~ *nutzlos*.**

From ~ the Scots *feck*, meaning *effect* – so literally, *effectless*.

If you like this word, try ~ fecund.

'If ye miss that, ye must be as feckless at the sailoring as I have found ye at the fighting' – Robert Louis Stevenson, *Kidnapped*

* See *Reckless*.
** Literally *nutless*.***
*** Not really.

FORAGE

foh-rij

Rhymes with ~ porridge.

Means ~ to search for, wander around looking for something.

As in ~ In the fading light, badgers emerge to forage for wild Gruyère.*

And ~ I forage down the back of the sofa for the TV remote, but all I find is a slice of old pizza.

A bit like ~ scavenge, rummage.

Almost an anagram of ~ fromage.**

---

* Named after the town of the same name in Switzerland, Gruyère is renowned as one of the finest cheeses for baking and particularly suited to fondues.
** French for *cheese*.

FRUGAL

froo-gul

Means ~ sparing, avoiding waste.

As in ~ When my teacher asks why I haven't done my homework I reply that I'm being frugal with ink.

And ~ In the olden days* people were more frugal and often shared trousers.**

A bit like ~ thrifty, prudent.

The opposite of ~ lavish, extravagant.

Don't confuse with ~ frugivore,*** or frogivore.****

WHOSE TROUSERS ARE THESE?

ANY REASON WHY WE HAVE ONLY ONE PAIR?

beats me...

---

*Any time before 2005.
Not at the same time, obviously.***
***An animal that eats mainly fruit.
****An animal that eats mainly frogs.
*****You think *that's* bad? I can remember a time when kids actually had to *share* computers and PlayStations with brothers and sisters instead of having one each!

FUTILE

few-tile

Means ~ pointless, no useful result.

As in ~ He tries to walk past the cheese counter* but resistance is futile.

And ~ It's futile asking for the latest Xbox for Christmas but I'm going to do it anyway.

A bit like ~ fruitless.

Nothing like ~ vegless.

The opposite of ~ worthwhile.

If you like this word, try ~ furore.

FRUITLESS

---

*That's *counter* as in *worktop* – not someone counting cheese.**
**That would be pretty futile.

GAMUT

gam-ut

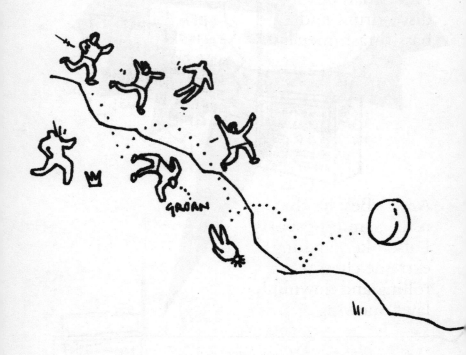

Means ~ the whole range of something.

A bit like ~ scale, scope.

As in ~ His taste in music ran the entire gamut of styles, from Paraguayan nose-flute orchestras to Hungarian death-disco-drum-and-bass-thrash-metal.

Don't confuse with ~ gambit,* or gannet.**

HOPE YOU ENJOYED THAT NOSE FLUTE, NOW IT'S TIME FOR SOME HUNGARIAN DEATH DISCO ON GAMUT FM!

And ~ Besides the usual gamut of sports I also like watching extreme cheese-rolling and downhill lawn-mowing.

---

*A kind of tactic, or move (in chess, for instance).
**A kind of seabird.

Rhymes with ~ wile.*

Means ~ cunning, craftiness.

As in ~ City's coach displayed a distinct lack of tactical guile by playing their goalie in attack for the first twenty minutes.

And ~ Their scheme to sell Grandma on eBay would take a considerable amount of guile if it was to succeed.

A bit like ~ slyness.

Don't confuse with ~ guillemot.**

In Norwegian ~ *svik*.

'Deep, hollow, treacherous, and full of guile'* –** William Shakespeare, *Richard III*

---

*Which funnily enough also means *trick*, or *cunning behaviour*.****
**A kind of seabird.
***But apart from that a really nice bloke.
****See *Circumvent*.*****
*****Also see Wile E. Coyote – one of the greatest cartoon characters of all time.

HAPLESS

hap-less

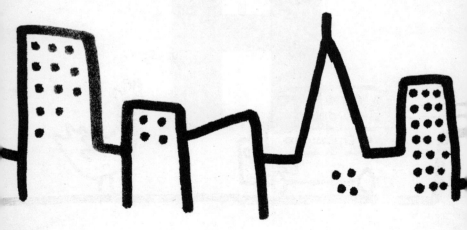

Means ~ unlucky.

As in ~ The hapless chicken eventually crosses the road but immediately gets run over.*

And ~ My hapless father finally fixes the car** but immediately runs over a chicken.***

A bit like ~ ill-fated, pitiful.

The opposite of ~ fortunate.

Don't confuse with ~ harpless.****

*But *why* did the chicken cross the road?
**See *Feckless*.
***No chickens were run over during the writing of this book.
****Means you've lost your harp.

HEINOUS

hay-nus

TOILETS

Rhymes with ~ Uranus.*

Means ~ shockingly wicked.

As in ~ The evil baddie's plan to steal Birmingham was not only heinous but also very stupid.**

And ~ To suggest that I *deliberately* missed the toilet and peed on the cat is a heinous accusation.

A bit like ~ atrocious, horrendous.

In German ~ *verabscheuungs-würdig.****

---

* Depending how you pronounce it!
** Where would he put it?
*** Anagram of 'another very long German word'.****
**** Not really.

HIATUS

hi-ate-us

R·I·P

REST IN
CHICKEN
PIECES

2010 ~ 2011

dead

Means ~ gap, pause.

As in ~ It's a pity the chicken didn't wait for a hiatus in the traffic before crossing the road.*

And ~ There was a hiatus in the meal while Dad changed his trousers.**

A bit like ~ interval, lull.

Don't confuse with ~ Haiti.***

From ~ the Latin *hiare*, meaning *gap*, or *to gape*.

Don't cross

Cross

Fowl road safety, fig. 1

---

*See *Hapless*.
**See *Condone*.
***There's an easy way of remembering the difference between *hiatus* and *Haiti*. One is an island in the Caribbean – and the other isn't.

HYPOCRITICAL

hippo-kritty-kal

I'M TWO FACED ...GET IT?

Means ~ saying one thing and doing another.*

As in ~ The hypocritical footballer kisses his shirt badge hours before signing for another team.

And ~ It was a bit hypocritical of Mum to tell me not to talk with my mouth full when she had her mouth full.

Don't confuse with ~ hypothetical,** or typocritical.***

A bit like ~ two-faced.

Nothing to do with ~ a seriously ill hippo.

* Or the other way round.
** Means *supposed*, or *theoretical*.
*** Means your finger slipped when you were typing *hypocritical*.

IGNOMINIOUS

ig-no-mini-us

Means ~ shameful, disgraceful.

As in ~ Thanks to their hapless goalie,* feckless defence** and indolent centre forward,*** the team were heading for a crushing and ignominious defeat.

And ~ Her attempt to eat a banana sideways ends in ignominious failure.

A bit like ~ inglorious, humiliating.

The opposite of ~ honourable.

If you like this word, try ~ ignoramus.

---

*See *Hapless*.
**See *Feckless*.
***See *Indolent*.

IMMATERIAL

im-ma-tea-real

i ideas. 27;

q um... 81

3)243

3)729

Means ~ unimportant, irrelevant.

As in ~ The impressive choice of vegetables on offer was immaterial as he had no intention of eating any of them.

And ~ I try telling my teacher it's immaterial what the square root of 729 is, but she insists I work it out anyway.*

A bit like ~ neither here nor there.

The opposite of ~ significant.

If you like this word, try ~ immutable.

*It's 27 in case you're wondering.**
**Or even if you're not.

IMPETUOUS

im-pet-you-us

Means ~ spur-of-the-moment, acting without thought.

As in ~ It was an impetuous decision to eat the banana sideways.*

And ~ It wasn't a great idea to stage-dive during assembly but the head teacher was feeling impetuous.

A bit like ~ impulsive, spontaneous.

Nothing like ~ a chain of pet shops.

The opposite of ~ cautious, premeditated.

Don't confuse with ~ tempestuous.**

In Finnish ~ *hätiköivä*.

'Few things are brought to a successful issue by impetuous desire, but most by calm and prudent* forethought'** – Thucydides

---

*See *Ignominious*.
**Stormy.
***Wise, careful.

INDOLENT

in-doh-lent

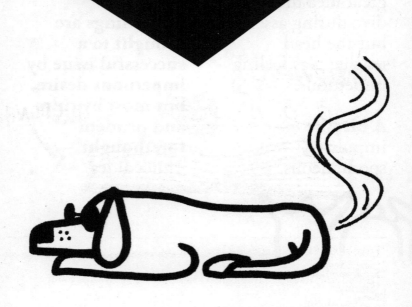

Means ~ lazy.

As in ~ The indolent dog lies in the sun, passing time and gas in equal measures.

And ~ Mum told me to look up 'indolent' in the dictionary but I couldn't be bothered.

A bit like ~ lethargic, slothful.*

Don't confuse with ~ redolent.**

'Indolence is the dry rot of even a good mind' – Tryon Edwards***

TUMBLEWEED

DICTIONARY

---

*From sloth – a creature *so* indolent that stuff actually grows on it!
**See *Redolent*
Mind rot? You need Thinkseal – stops leaky brains or your money back!*
****Terms and conditions apply.

Means ~ stubborn, obstinate.

As in ~ My intransigent teacher insists I work out the square root of 729.*

And ~ I hammer on the toilet door but my intransigent dad refuses to budge.

A bit like ~ obdurate.

The opposite of ~ flexible.

Anagram of ~ tennis gratin.**

Don't confuse with ~ incontinent.***

---

*See *Immaterial*.****

** Like ordinary tennis but with a topping of cheese.

*** You'll have to look that up yourself. But I'll give you a clue. It's got nothing to do with continents.

**** It's still 27 in case you're still wondering.*****

***** Or even if you're still not.

INTREPID

in-trep-id

Means ~
fearless, bold.

As in ~ The intrepid
wildebeest stares at
the lion with barely
concealed disdain.*

And ~ The intrepid
explorer** finally
reaches the Lost City
of Youtubia but it's
closed.***

A bit like ~
courageous,
audacious.

Anagram of ~
tip diner.****

**Don't confuse
with ~** insipid.*****

* Means to look down your nose at someone or something. No mean feat
if you're a wildebeest.
** If you want to be an explorer you *have* to be intrepid. It's the first
thing they ask you at the interview.
*** Even more annoyingly it also turned out to be completely fictional.
**** Something a waiter or waitress should always do if they're satisfied
with the way someone has eaten their meal.
***** Dull, flavourless.

93

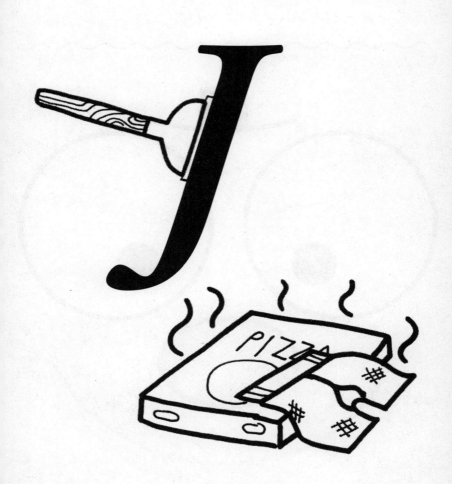

JOCULAR

jock-u-lar

Means ~ humorous.*

As in ~
Fortunately the lecture on 19th-century Belgian plumbing techniques contained a number of jokes** and jocular remarks.

And ~ Uncle Frank was his usual jocular self until he arrived home to discover his conservatory had been destroyed by a meteorite.

A bit like ~ waggish, whimsical.

In Swedish ~ *skämtsam*.

From ~ the Latin *joculus*, meaning *little joke*.***

---

*Don't confuse *humorous* with *hummus* – the popular Middle Eastern dish made from chick peas, tahini, garlic, olive oil and a dash of lemon juice.
**How many 19th-century Belgian plumbers does it take to change a washer? Just one, providing they've undergone the necessary training.
As opposed to *cookulus*, meaning *Little Chef*.*
****Not really.

JUNCTURE

junk-chur

Rhymes with ~ puncture.

Means ~ point in time – usually a vital one.

As in ~ Talks between the footballer and his hairdresser had reached a critical juncture.

And ~ It was at that juncture she decided her sister truly was the spawn* of Satan.

A bit like ~ moment, stage.

Can also mean ~ the part of the body where two things are joined, e.g. the *juncture* between the oesophagus and the stomach epithelium.**

---

* As in *offspring*, not *frog*.
** But you probably knew that already.

JURISDICTION

jure-is-dik-shun

Means ~
power, authority.

As in ~ It's common
knowledge that the
lion has jurisdiction
in the jungle.*

And ~ It's common
knowledge that my
mum has jurisdiction
in our house.

A bit like ~
control, influence.

Anagram of ~
I snot juridic.**

*The lion's more natural habitat is actually the grasslands of southern
Africa – but somehow 'King of the Grasslands' just doesn't have the same
ring to it.
Pretty meaningless, but a good excuse to use the word *snot*.*
***Not to be sniffed at.

JUXT·POSE

jux-ta-pose

Means ~ to place side by side – often for the purposes of comparison or contrast.

As in ~ The famous artist juxtaposes a fish and a toilet seat and is told he's a genius.

And ~ I juxtapose an old pizza box and some pants and am told I'm repugnant.*

A bit like ~ put next to.

Rhymes with ~ absolutely zilch.**

Not ~ the Latin for *just suppose*.

Or ~ the Latin for *in a bit*.***

---

*See *Repugnant*.
**Nothing!
That's *juxtaminute*.*
****Not really.

KOWTOW

cow-tow[*]

Means ~ to suck up to, or bow down to someone.

As in ~ The cheese shop owner refuses to kowtow to the customer until she can prove she really is the Queen.**

And ~ I'd rather drink my own puke than kowtow to my sister.

A bit like ~ grovel, toady.

From ~ the Mandarin *Kòu tóu*, meaning *knock head* (on ground as a sign of respect).***

HAVE YOU SEEN MY TOWEL?

---

*That's *cow* as in large animal with dangly bits and *tow* as in the first bit of *town*, or *towel*.
**How's she supposed to do that? Show them a stamp?
***Don't try that at home, kids.

KUDOS

cue-dos

Means ~ praise or acclaim – usually for a particular achievement.

As in ~ Grandpa achieved considerable kudos at the allotments for the size of his marrows.

And ~ Knowing someone who knows someone whose Granny's next-door neighbour's second cousin was on *The X Factor* gave me instant kudos in the playground.

A bit like ~ status, prestige.

Don't confuse with ~ a kind of aftershave.*

Not quite an anagram of ~ sudoku.

---

*'Kudos pour homme!'**
**Try saying that in a breathy French accent like they do on the telly and you'll see what I mean.

LOQUACIOUS

low-kway-shus

Means ~
very talkative.

A bit like ~
garrulous, voluble.**

As in ~
His loquacious
good humour was
infectious,* but
sadly so was his
chickenpox.

And also ~
logorrhoea.***

The opposite of ~
taciturn.****

And ~ The more
sherry trifle she ate,
the more loquacious
Grandma became.

---

*Catching.
**Don't confuse *voluble* with *volleyball*.
Means *excessive talkativeness*.**
****See *Taciturn*.
*****Don't confuse *logorrhoea* with *diarrhoea*.******
******Means excessive . . . On second thoughts, let's not go there.

Means ~
spiteful, wishing
harm on others.

As in ~
The malevolent
elephant squishes
the squirrel.*

And ~ My baby
sister's malevolent
gaze chills me to the
bone.

A bit like ~
malicious, vindictive.

The opposite of ~
benevolent.

Don't confuse ~ a
malevolent elephant
with an *irrelevant*
elephant.**

In Lithuanian –
piktdžiugiškas.

**'Miss Pross knew
full well that
Madame Defarge
was the family's
malevolent enemy'**
– Charles Dickens,
A Tale of Two Cities

---

*No squirrels were squished
during the writing of this book.
**See *Immaterial*.

MENDACIOUS

men-day-shus

Means – untruthful, lying.

As in ~ The mendacious Big Bad Wolf only pretends to be on a revolutionary new pig-free diet.

And ~ I wasn't being *deliberately* mendacious when Mum asked if I'd cleaned my teeth – I thought she meant had I *ever* cleaned them!*

A bit like ~ deceitful, duplicitous.

The opposite of ~ honest.

In Latin ~ *fibbius porkium.***

Anagram of ~ nude mosaic.

---

*See *Misconstrued*.
**Not really, I'm being *mendacious*.

MISCONSTRUED

mis-cons-trood

Means ~
misunderstood
the meaning.

As in ~ The
footballer claims the
ref misconstrued his
hand gesture and
that he was merely
pointing out he'd
scored two goals.

And ~ The dog
misconstrued its
owner and ate
the stick.

A bit like ~
misinterpreted.

The opposite of ~
comprehended.

In Norwegian ~
*misforstå.**

Anagram of ~
cistern modus.**

*Don't confuse *misforstå* with Miss *Forster.***
**A state-of-the-art toilet.
***My old maths teacher.

MUNDANE

mun-dane

Means ~ ordinary, unremarkable, boring.

As in ~ Despite the special effects and heavy-metal soundtrack, the fly-on-the-wall documentary series about the firm of accountants was still somewhat mundane.

And ~ He was beginning to find the whole getting-up-and-going-to-school thing a bit mundane.

A bit like ~ humdrum, banal.

From ~ the Latin *mundus*, meaning *world*.*

Don't confuse with – someone from Mundania.**

THIS PAGE IS PROPER BORING...

*Mundane can also mean *wordly*, or *relating to the world*.
**A country in Eastern Europe that I've just made up.

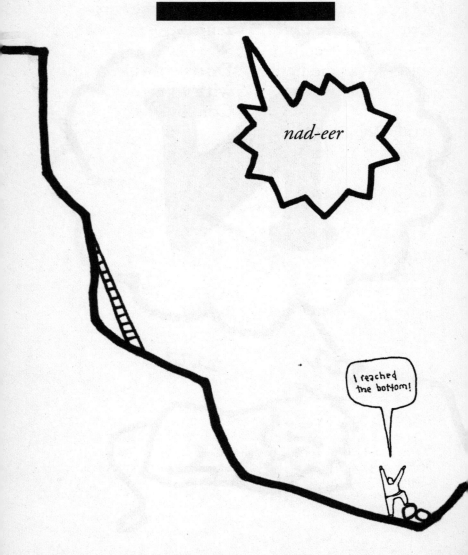

Means ~ lowest point.

As in ~ Getting sent off before the match had even started was the nadir of his career.

And ~ Some say Saturday night TV reached an all-time nadir with *Celebrity Strictly Come Strictly Dine with Me Strictly on Ice.**

A bit like ~ the pits, rock bottom.

The opposite of ~ zenith.

Don't confuse with ~ Nadia Comăneci.**

*But they're wrong.***
**Famous Romanian gymnast.
The actual nadir was *Celebrity Strictly Come Strictly Dine with Me Strictly on Ice EXTRA*, which followed straight after on the other channel.*
****In my opinion.*****
*****See *Dogmatic*.

NEBULOUS

neb-you-lus

Means ~
vague, unclear.

As in ~ The reasons
my sister gave for
suddenly demanding
all my pocket money
were rather nebulous.

And ~ I try telling
my teacher that I
find the concept of
equations somewhat
nebulous but she
insists that I do
them anyway.

A bit like ~
hazy, murky.

The opposite of ~
precise, distinct.

From ~
The Latin *nebula*,
meaning *cloud*.

Anagram of ~
Olé! Un bus!*

*Spanish for 'Hurrah! A bus!'**
**Possibly.

129

NONCHALANT

non-show-lent

••

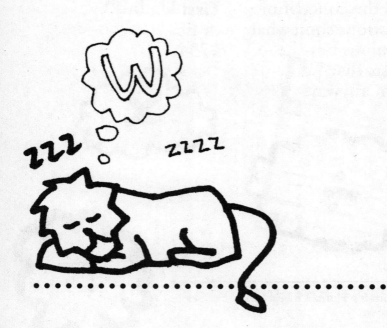

Means ~
casual, cool.

As in ~
The nonchalant
wildebeest
saunters past
the sleeping lion.

And ~ I feel
surprisingly
nonchalant as Mum
reads my report card.

A bit like ~ laid-
back, unconcerned.

The opposite of ~
anxious.

From ~ The old
French word
nonchaloir, meaning
to be unconcerned.

First known use ~
in England, about
1734.*

---

* Presumably things just weren't very cool before then.

OBSOLETE

ob-so-leet

Means ~ outdated, not used any more.

As in ~ Grandpa was devastated to find his all-time favourite breakfast cereal, Cheesy Bix, was now obsolete.*

And ~ By the time my dad works out how to use his new phone it'll be obsolete.

A bit like ~ archaic, old hat.

The opposite of ~ contemporary.

If you like this word, try ~ obliterate.

OLD HAT

---

*Other cheese-based breakfast cereals are available.

OBSTREPEROUS

obs-trep-er-us

Means ~ unruly, difficult to control.

As in ~ The longer he spent playing *World of Grand Tomb Theft Apocalypse 6*, the more obstreperous he became.*

And ~ My obstreperous cousins make a bunch of hyperactive baboons seem shy and reserved by comparison.

A bit like ~ boisterous, raucous.

The opposite of ~ placid, docile.

Probably ~ where the word *stroppy*** comes from.

If you like this word, try ~ cantankerous.

---

*See *Underwhelmed.*
**See teenagers.

OSTENTATIOUS

os-ten-tay-shus

Means ~
showy, flash.

As in ~ The
footballer's house
was so ostentatious
that each en-suite
bathroom had
its own en-suite
bathroom.

And ~ The
ostentatious celebrity
drops her kids off at
school by helicopter.*

A bit like ~
pretentious, swanky.

The opposite of ~
modest, reserved.

**Don't confuse
with ~** Austin, Texas.

**'He welcomed them
a second time,
with ostentatious
formality to his
humble abode'** –
Jane Austen, *Pride
and Prejudice***

---

*That's *by* helicopter – not *from* a helicopter.
Ostent*atious? *Austin*, Texas? Jane *Austen*? Coincidence?
****Definitely.

PENCHANT

Means ~ a strong liking or taste for something.

As in ~ Grandpa has a penchant for Cheesy Bix.*

And ~ My little brother has a penchant for bugging the heck out of me.

A bit like ~ fondness, predilection.

The opposite of ~ aversion.

In French ~ *penchant*.

Don't confuse with ~ poncho.**

NOT A PONCHO!

---

*Or at least he did until it became obsolete.***
Cape-like item of clothing from South America.**
***See *Obsolete*.
****Peruvians in particular have a penchant for ponchos.

PETULANT

Means ~
rude, irritable.

As in ~ The petulant
footballer reacts
to his red card by
sticking his tongue
out at the ref.

And ~ Having a
tantrum in the
middle of the
supermarket was
the kind of petulant
behaviour I'd come
to expect from
my dad.

A bit like ~ insolent.

Nothing like ~ a
chain of pet shops.*

**'"What is it all
about?" cried
Dorian in his
petulant way,
flinging himself
down on the sofa'**
– Oscar Wilde, *The
Picture of Dorian
Gray*

HE'S NOT
WITH ME...

---

*Oops – I've done that gag already.**
See *Impetuous*.*
See – told you I recycled jokes!*
****See *Expeditious*.

PHENOMENAL

fen-om-en-al*

Means ~ extraordinary, remarkable.

As in ~ For a small dog it produced a phenomenal amount of gas.

And ~ Wearing the same pair of pants for a whole year was a phenomenal achievement.**

A bit like ~ prodigious, unparalleled.

The opposite of ~ average.

In Icelandic ~ *stórkostlegum.*

If you like this word, try ~ prestigious.

---

*The 'p' is silent as in *bath*.****
Not to mention *reckless* and *repugnant*.*
***See *Reckless* and *Repugnant*.
****Geddit? Pee? Silent? As in *bath*?

PLETHORA

pleth-or-a

PLETHORA PLETHORA PLETHORA PLETHORA PLETHORA PLETHORA
PLETHORA PLETHORA PLETHORA PLETHORA PLETHORA PLETHORA
PLETHORA PLETHORA PLETHORA PLETHORA PLETHORA PLETHORA
PLETHORA PLETHORA PLETHORA PLETHORA PLETHORA PLETHORA
PLETHORA PLETHORA PLETHORA PLETHORA PLETHORA PLETHORA
PLETHORA PLETHORA PLETHORA PLETHORA PLETHORA PLETHORA
PLETHORA PLETHORA PLETHORA PLETHORA PLETHORA PLETHORA
PLETHORA PLETHORA PLETHORA PLETHORA PLETHORA PLETHORA
PLETHORA PLETHORA PLETHORA PLETHORA PLETHORA PLETHORA
PLETHORA PLETHORA PLETHORA PLETHORA PLETHORA PLETHORA
PLETHORA PLETHORA PLETHORA PLETHORA PLETHORA PLETHORA
PLETHORA PLETHORA PLETHORA PLETHORA PLETHORA PLETHORA
PLETHORA PLETHORA PLETHORA PLETHORA PLETHORA PLETHORA
PLETHORA PLETHORA PLETHORA PLETHORA PLETHORA PLETHORA
PLETHORA PLETHORA PLETHORA PLETHORA PLETHORA PLETHORA
PLETHORA PLETHORA PLETHORA PLETHORA PLETHORA PLETHORA
PLETHORA PLETHORA PLETHORA PLETHORA PLETHORA PLETHORA
PLETHORA PLETHORA PLETHORA PLETHORA PLETHORA PLETHORA
PLETHORA PLETHORA PLETHORA PLETHORA PLETHORA PLETHORA
PLETHORA PLETHORA PLETHORA PLETHORA PLETHORA PLETHORA
PLETHORA PLETHORA PLETHORA PLETHORA PLETHORA PLETHORA

A PLETHORA OF PLETHORAS

Means ~ large amount, surplus of something.

As in ~ There was a plethora of movies about dragons and wizards, but only one about zombie badgers from Mars.*

And ~ I can think of a plethora of reasons for not doing my homework, but none which my teacher would actually believe.**

A bit like ~ glut, overabundance.

The opposite of ~ dearth.***

Don't confuse with ~ plethodon.****

From ~ the Greek *plethore*, meaning *full*.*****

ZOMBIE BADGER FROM MARS

YES, REALLY

Zombie Badgers From Mars. Went straight to DVD.
**Attack by zombie badgers from Mars presumably being one of them.
***See *Dearth*.
****A kind of lizard.
*****So next time you're offered something to eat that you don't like, just say, 'No thanks, I'm *plethore*.'

PROCRASTINATE

pro-cras-ti-nate

Means ~ deliberately put off doing something.*

As in ~ It's a pity the chicken didn't procrastinate a bit longer before crossing the road.**

And ~ I choose to procrastinate in my room rather than actually tidy it.

A bit like ~ stall for time, dilly-dally.

Nothing like ~ the word before *procrastinine*.***

If you like this word, try ~ prevaricate.

'Procrastination is the thief of time' – Edward Young

*Usually something boring or unpleasant.
**See *Hapless*.
Oops, there I go again, recycling jokes.*
****See *Asinine*.

151

QUALMS

kwaarms

Rhymes with ~ charms.

Means ~ doubts, uneasy feelings about something you're about to do.

As in ~ My brother has no qualms about changing channels without asking first.

And ~ I'll have no qualms about hitting him if he does it again.

A bit like ~ misgivings, scruples.

Don't confuse with ~ the qualm before the storm.*

'No quarrel with silence; no qualms with vigilance'** – Hindu proverb

---

*The actual expression is 'the *calm* before the storm'.***

**Vigilance* means *watchfulness*.

Funnily enough though, a qualm can also mean a feeling of sickness or nausea – which you may *well* get before a storm!*

****Bet you're glad I brought *that* up!

Means ~ state of uncertainty or indecision.

As in ~ Faced with such a plethora* of cheese, he was in a quandary which one to choose.

And ~ I'm in a quandary whether to play *World of Grand Tomb Theft Apocalypse 6* or watch *Celebrity Strictly Come Strictly Dine with Me Strictly on Ice.*

A bit like ~ dilemma, predicament.

Don't confuse ~ being in a *quandary* with being in a *quarry.***

In Slovakian ~ *pochybnosti.*

If you like this word, try ~ quagmire.

you will need this for your nose.

---

* See *Plethora.*
** You might find yourself *in* one if you fall in the other!

RECKLESS

Means ~ having no thought of possible consequences.

As in ~ It was reckless of the zebra to stray too close to the crocodile.*

And ~ It was reckless of me to go to the toilet straight after my dad.

A bit like ~ negligent, rash.

Nothing to do with ~ a lack of sunken ships.

The opposite of ~ cautious.

Don't confuse with ~ feckless.**

ARE YOU TALKING TO ME?

*See *Truncated*.
**See *Feckless*.

REDOLENT

red-oh-lent

Means ~ suggestive of, smelling of.

As in ~ Grandpa's house was redolent of cherished memories and faded dreams.*

And ~ The school hall was redolent of floor polish and stale farts.**

A bit like ~ evocative, reminiscent.

In Spanish ~ *oliente.*

Don't confuse with ~ indolent.***

'And on the spectral mountain's crown, The wearied light is dying down, And earth, and stars, and sea, and sky, Are redolent of sleep'
– Edgar Allan Poe****

*Pretty profound eh?*****
**Not quite so profound.
***See *Indolent.*
****Clearly no Dizzee Rascal.
*****Intense, deep, meaningful.

REMONSTRATE

rem-on-strate

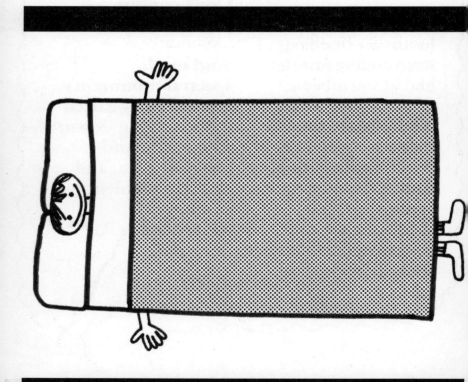

Means ~ argue, plead.

A bit like ~ protest, dispute.

As in ~ The footballer briefly stops rolling around like he's just been shot in order to remonstrate with the ref.

In Italian ~ *rimostranze*.

Anagram of ~ etna tremors.**

And ~ I remonstrate about the futility* of making my bed when I'm only going to sleep in it again later.

* See *Futile*.
** A volcano in Sicily.***
*** Nothing whatsoever to do with *remonstrate* – I just thought it was quite interesting.

*ren-eg or ren-aig**

Means ~ break a promise, back out.

As in ~ My parents renege on their agreement not to be embarrassing by snogging in the middle of the supermarket.

And ~ I renege on my promise to only pee in the toilet.**

A bit like ~ revoke, default.

The opposite of ~ adhering, sticking to something.

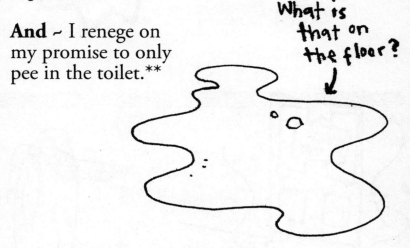

What is that on the floor?

---

* It means exactly the same thing whichever way you pronounce it.***
** See *Heinous*.
*** There are some words that mean different things depending on how you pronounce them. For instance, you can *row* a boat (as in *paddle*) – or you can have a *row* with someone (as in *argument*).****
**** Next time you read about two people *rowing* in a boat, don't automatically assume all is well!

REPUGNANT

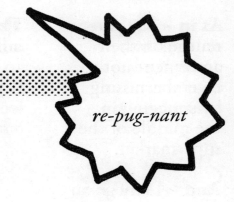

re-pug-nant

Means ~ disgusting, gross.

As in ~ The smell wafting from under her brother's door was utterly repugnant.

And ~ They used to be my favourite boy/girl band* but now I find them repugnant.

A bit like ~ repulsive, obnoxious.

The opposite of ~ innocuous.

If you like this word, try ~ refulgent.

---

*Delete where not applicable.**

In your head. Don't actually delete. Especially if you borrowed this book from a library.*

You don't want to mess with a librarian. They may seem like a quiet and mild-mannered bunch, but many are experts in the martial art of Thai Booksing.*

****Like Thai *Boxing* – but instead of kicking someone you throw a book at them.*****

*****But I digress.******

*******Digress* means *stray from the subject*.*******

*******Sorry about all these asterisks.********

********The little star shapes.

RUSE

rooz

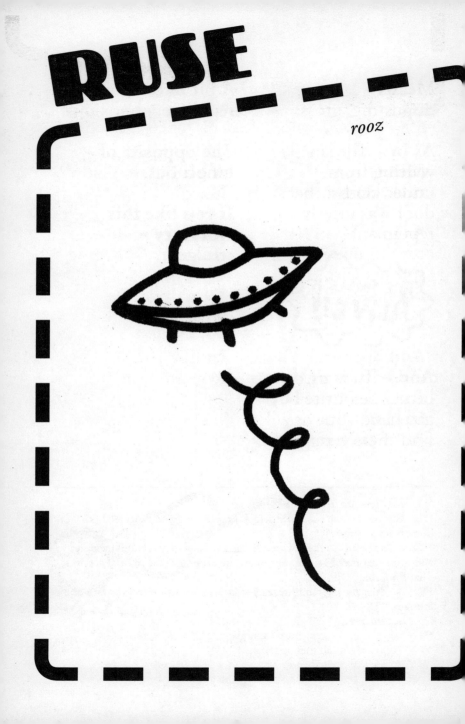

Means ~
trick, dodge.

As in ~ Mum's
ruse to mix puréed
sprouts with the
mashed potato fools
no one.

And ~ It turned out
Grandpa hadn't been
abducted by aliens
after all – it was all
just a cunning ruse.

A bit like ~ ploy,
hoax.

Rhymes with ~
muse.*

**Don't confuse
with** ~ ruse.**

In Spanish ~
artimaña.

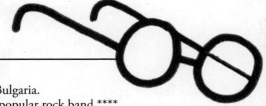

---

*Ponder, mull over.***
**Fifth largest city in Bulgaria.
Also the name of a popular rock band.*
****As well as the name given in Greek mythology to any of the nine
daughters of Zeus and Mnemosyne.*****
*****Mnemosyne was the goddess of memory who . . .******
******Sorry – can't remember what I was going to say.

SANGUINE

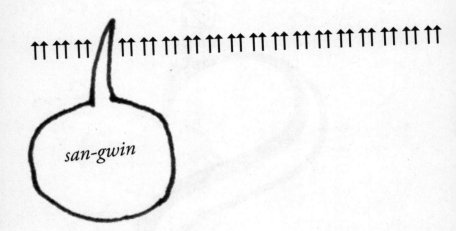

san-gwin

HANG ON...
A WHA...
A WHAT
SANDWICH?!

Things are looking up!

Means ~ confident, hopeful.

As in ~ Despite their team losing 8–0 at half-time, the fans remained remarkably sanguine.

And ~ I'm sanguine about my chances of a decent report as long as I manage to bribe the teachers first.*

A bit like ~ optimistic, upbeat.

Not ~ another name for a penguin sandwich.

From ~ the Latin *sanguis*, meaning blood.**

'His sanguine spirit turns every firefly into a star' – Arthur Conan Doyle

---

*Obviously I'm not *condoning* such behaviour.****

In the olden days people with ruddy or *sanguine* complexions were thought to be more cheerful.*

***Perhaps they just needed the toilet.

****See *Condone*.

SKEDADDLE

ski-da-dull

Means ~ to flee, clear off in a panic.*

As in ~ Mistaking the sound of an approaching ice-cream van for the sound of a police car, the youths skedaddle.

And ~ I skedaddle, leaving my little brother holding the empty biscuit tin.

A bit like ~ scarper, run for the hills.**

In Chinese ~ 不及物动词.

If you liked this word, try ~ shenanigans.

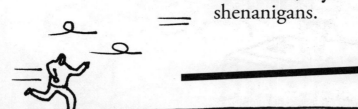

*Usually from the scene of a misdemeanour.***
**Running for the hills is not generally recommended in The Netherlands since there aren't any.
***Wrongdoing, or minor misdeed.

SURREPTITIOUS

Surreptitious as a fox

Means ~ secret, sly.

As in ~ *The X Factor* contestant regrets taking a surreptitious swig of Coke just before she walks on stage.*

And ~ Standing in the crowded lift, I release a surreptitious trouser cough.**

A bit like ~ sneaky, stealthy.

The opposite of ~ conspicuous, blatant.

Don't confuse with ~ serendipitous.***

'Surreptitious fishes avoid dishes' – Old Mundanian proverb****

surr-up-tish-us

ME? ON A DISH, BRUV?? PAH!

---

*Other burp-inducing fizzy drinks are available.
**Bottom burp.
***Lucky – which is more than can be said for the other folk in the lift.
****See *Mundane*.

TACITURN

tassy-turn

Means ~ untalkative.

As in ~ His taciturn nature, his hatred of sport and his chronic inability to remember names were all unusual qualities in a football commentator.*

And ~ When I heard myself described as taciturn I was lost for words.

A bit like ~ reserved, reticent.

The opposite of ~ loquacious.**

In German ~ *schweigsam*.

If you like this word, try ~ tactile.

'The dead keep their secrets, and in a while we shall be as wise as they – and as taciturn' – Alexander Smith, nineteenth-century poet***

---

* 'I think someone's scored but I'm not sure who. Oh, who cares, frankly?'
** See *Loquacious*.
*** Sounds like a bundle of laughs.

TRAVESTY

trav-es-tee

Means ~ exaggerated imitation.

As in ~ The footballer's claim that he *deliberately* fell over and let the ball bounce off his backside and into the goal was a travesty of the truth.

And ~ Making me cut the lawn with a pair of scissors just because I threw a stick of celery at my sister was a travesty of justice.*

A bit like ~ mockery, sham.

From ~ the French *travestir*, meaning *to disguise*.

---

* Fair enough if it had been a potato or a bit of broccoli. But I mean, come on! *Celery?*

TRUNCATED

trunk-ate-ed

Means ~ cut short.

As in ~ The zebra's lifespan is severely truncated when it strays too close to the crocodile.*

And ~ Christmas dinner was suddenly truncated when the dog ran away with the turkey.**

A bit like ~ curtailed, abbreviated.

Nothing to do with ~ being whacked by an elephant.

The opposite of ~ lengthened.

If you like this word, try ~ truculent.

---

*No zebras were harmed during the writing of this book.
Hey, if a dish can run away with a spoon,* a dog can run away with a turkey!
***See *Cahoots*.

UBIQUITOUS

Means ~ being, or seeming to be, everywhere at the same time.

As in ~ The ubiquitous film star stares moodily from the side of every bus.

And ~ My teacher is so ubiquitous I'm beginning to think he's been cloned.

A bit like ~ omnipresent, universal.

Don't confuse with ~ *biquitous digesticum.** *

In Dutch ~ *alomtegenwoordige.*

UBIQUI-
TEACH
400L.2

RAAAAAAAA!!

THIS ONE'S
GONE BONKERS!

*Latin for *digestive biscuit.** *
As opposed to *creamicus custium.* *
***Latin for custard cream.

MMM...
Just one more.

UNCTUOUS

unk-choo-us

Means ~ smug, insincere.

As in ~ The unctuous comedian laughs at his own jokes even when no one else does.

And ~ Seeing my unctuous uncle flirt with my best friend's mum makes me want to lose my lunch.*

A bit like ~ gushing, smarmy.

The opposite of ~ genuine.

In Swedish ~ *salvelsefull*.

If you like this word, try ~ sumptuous.

---

*Barf.**
Hurl.*
Puke.*
****You get the idea.

UNDERWHELMED

—

un-der-welmed

Means ~ unimpressed, disappointed by something.

As in ~ Dad was underwhelmed by my sister's attempt to paint the car.

FLOWERY PAINT

And ~ After all the build-up and hype I'm left distinctly underwhelmed by *World of Grand Tomb Theft Apocalypse 7.**

A bit like ~ cool, unexcited.

The opposite of ~ overwhelmed.****

Anagram of ~ demur when led.*****

---

*Any similarity between *World of Grand Tomb Theft Apocalypse 7* and an actual game is completely on purpose.
**Duh.
***See *Demur*.

UNDETERRED

*undie-turd**

Means ~ not put off from doing something.

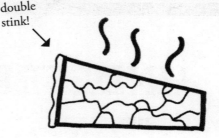

double stink!

As in ~ Undeterred by his severe cheese allergy, he orders the Gruyère and Stilton pie.**

A bit like ~ undiscouraged, not dissuaded.

The opposite of ~ overterred.****

And ~ Despite even their own families telling them that they're rubbish,*** the boy band remain undeterred and audition for *The X Factor*.

Don't confuse with ~ disinterred.*****

stink ⟶

---

*Yeah, yeah, very funny.

Not to be recommended.****

***Whoa – they really *must've* been bad!

****Just joking. The opposite of *undeterred* is actually *deterred*. (Duh!)

*****Means *dug up a dead body*.

******I don't mean I'm not recommending the Gruyère and Stilton pie. I mean I don't recommend ordering it if you have a severe cheese allergy!

Is that a
vildebeest?!

VEHEMENTLY

veer-ment-lee

The hand of
my brother

Last biscuit

Means ~ strongly, forcefully.

As in ~ I vehemently oppose my brother's suggestion that he should have the last chocolate biscuit.

And ~ My brother protests vehemently when I take the last chocolate biscuit.*

A bit like ~ fervently, emphatically.

The opposite of ~ calmly, impassively.

Anagram of ~ helmet envy.**

---

*Note that *vehemently* is usually followed by quite negative words like *oppose*, *deny* and *protest*. Only very rarely do you hear someone say that they 'vehemently like kittens'.***
**An increasingly common condition among cyclists.
Come to think of it, I've *never* heard someone say that they vehemently like kittens.*
****Puppies, yes. But kittens? Never.

VERVE

vuurve

Rhymes with ~ luurve.

Means ~ enthusiasm, energy.

As in ~ Grandpa polished off the cheeseboard with his customary verve.*

And ~ According to my teacher my essay not only lacked verve it also lacked structure punctuation grammar adjectives and any kind of sense whatsoever which was like well not good right?

A bit like ~ vigour, vitality.

Don't confuse with ~ vervet.**

The opposite of ~ apathy, torpor.

If you like this word, try ~ Vivacious.

---

*Meaning that he ate all the cheese *on* the board – not the actual board.
**A small black-faced monkey, common in Eastern and Southern Africa.

VORACIOUS

vore-ay-shus

Means ~
exceptionally hungry,
especially keen on
something.

As in ~ The
voracious lion
devours the
wildebeest.*

And ~ My voracious
appetite for cheesy
TV is matched only
by my voracious
appetite for cheese.

A bit like ~
ravenous, insatiable.

From ~ the Latin
vorare, meaning
swallow.**

**Don't confuse
with ~** veracious.***

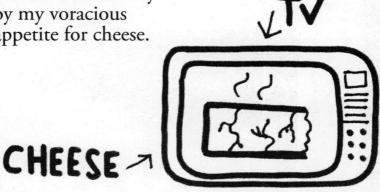

*It had it coming.****
**As in *devour*, not *bird*.
***Truthful, accurate.
****See *Circumvent, Discombobulate, Intrepid* and *Nonchalant*.

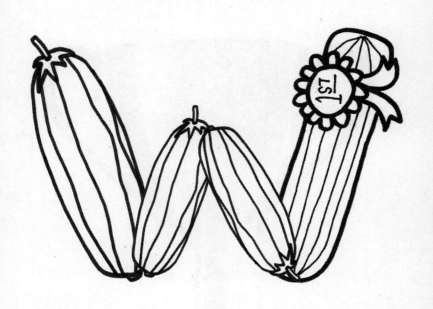

WISTFUL

wist-full

Means ~ full of regretful longing.

As in ~ Grandpa becomes misty-eyed and wistful when recalling his prize-winning marrows.*

And ~ The author gazes at his son's mop of luxuriant** hair with a wistful expression.

A bit like ~ pensive, melancholic.

In Hungarian ~ *vágyakozó*.

'I never saw a man who looked With such a wistful eye Upon that little tent of blue Which prisoners call the sky' – Oscar Wilde

*See *Kudos*.
Thick and abundant. In other words the complete opposite to the author's own hair.*
Any similarity between the author portrayed in this completely made-up sentence and the author who wrote this book is entirely coincidental.*
****If you believe *that* you'll believe anything.*****
*****Like cheese-eating badgers and skateboarding wildebeest.

XENOPHOBIC

zen-o-fo-bik

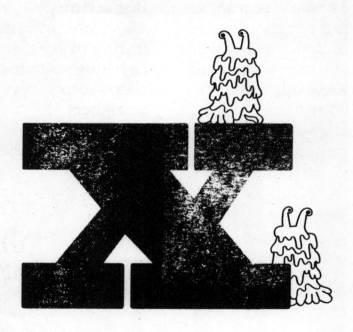

Means ~ that 'X' is pretty rubbish when it comes to big words you're ever likely to use while talking to your mates – which, after all, is the whole point of this book.*

But seriously ~ *xenophobic* means fearing or hating anything strange or alien – especially foreigners.**

Anagram of ~ ibex poncho.***

DON'T BE A HATER, BE A LOVER!

---

*See 'How to use this book and stuff' on page vii.
**And if you think I'm going to do a couple of funny sentences about that you've got another think coming!
A cape-like garment* worn by an ibex, or wild goat.
****See *Penchant*.

YEARN

yern

Rhymes with ~ stern.

Means ~ that when it comes to big words you could actually slip into normal, everyday conversation, 'Y' isn't that much better than 'X'!

But seriously ~ *yearn* means to long for, or have a strong desire for something or someone.*

As in ~ How I yearn to be an only child again.

And ~ Grandpa yearns for Cheesy Bix.**

A bit like ~ crave, hanker.

In Turkish ~ *özlemek.*

*See *Wistful.*
**See *Obsolete.*

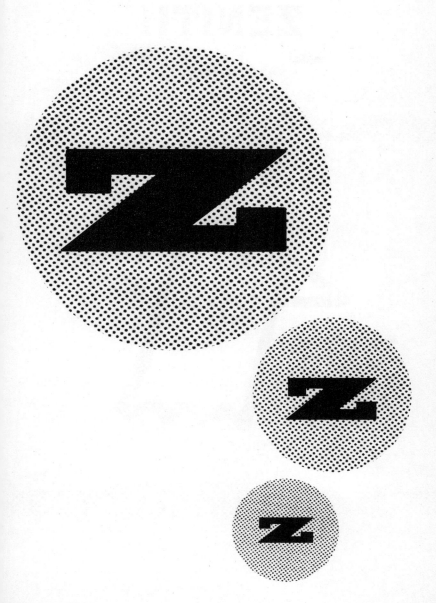

ZENITH

zen-ith

Means ~
highest point.

As in ~ Winning
Hairstyle of
the Year was the
zenith of the
footballer's career.

And ~ The boy
band's popularity
reached its zenith
when their cover
version of another
boy band's cover
version reached
Number 85 in
the charts.*

A bit like ~
peak, pinnacle.

The opposite of ~
nadir.**

**Don't confuse
with ~** Zenit St
Petersburg.***

Anagram of ~
hen zit.****

---

*Exactly the same number as the number of big words in this book.*****
**See *Nadir*.
***Top Russian football team.
****Another term for *chicken spot*.
*****Coincidence?******
******You decide.

IF YOU LIKE THOSE WORDS, TRY THESE!

ABATED ~ reduced in amount, decreased.

ASSIDUOUS ~ hard-working, persistent.

CANTANKEROUS ~ grumpy, bad-tempered.

CIRCUMSPECT ~ careful, cautious.

COHORT ~ companion, associate.

DIDACTIC ~ intended to teach, instruct.

FECUND ~ fertile, productive.

FURORE ~ uproar, commotion.

IGNORAMUS ~ an ignorant, uneducated person.

IMMUTABLE ~ unchanging, constant.

NINCOMPOOP ~ foolish person, idiot.

OBLITERATE ~ wipe out, destroy every trace.

PALAVER ~ a situation causing unnecessary trouble or hassle.

PRESTIGIOUS ~ impressive, renowned.

PREVARICATE ~ to stray from the truth, beat about the bush.

QUAGMIRE ~ literally *a bog*, but also a dilemma or difficult situation.

REFULGENT ~ shining, radiant.

SHENANIGANS ~ devious tricks, mischievous activities.

SUMPTUOUS ~ grand, luxurious.

TACTILE ~ relating to the sense of touch.

TRUCULENT ~ defiant, hostile.

VIVACIOUS ~ lively, sparkling.

PHiLiP ArdagH'S book OF

ABSOLUTELY

USELESS

LISTS

FOR aBSOLUTELY EVERY DaY OF THE YEaR

FaMoUS FictioNaL baLd FoLK, tHe
baSic reqUireMeNtS For beiNg a pirate
captaiN aNd everytHiNg yoU NeveR Need
to KNoW aboUt bUrpiNg – tHere'S a
USeLeSS LiSt For every day OF tHe
year iN tHiS bUMPer book.

PHiLip ArdagH HaS pLUNdered tHe
deepest corNerS OF HiS braiN to briNg
yoU a book aboUt NotHiNg, everytHiNg
aNd SoMetHiNg eLSe entireLy.

PHILIP Ardagh's book OF HOWLERS BLUNDERS and RANDOM MISTAKERY

Find out how the Pope got confused with a potato, about the footballer who ate the ref's notebook and why it's a terrible idea to get your name and date of birth tattooed on your neck in this splendid romp through the most impressive mistakes, blunders, misunderstandings, faux pas, howlers and universal truths that are not true at all!

A selected list of titles available from Macmillan Children's Books

The prices shown below are correct at the time of going to press. However, Macmillan Publishers reserves the right to show new retail prices on covers, which may differ from those previously advertised.

Philip Ardagh

Philip Ardagh's Book of Absolutely Useless Lists	978-0-330-43417-1	£6.99
Philip Ardagh's Book of Howlers, Blunders and Random Mistakery	978-0-330-50807-0	£5.99

Tony Robinson

Bad Kids	978-0-330-51080-6	£7.99

Glenn Murphy

Will Farts Destroy the Planet?	978-0-330-51770-6	£5.99

All Pan Macmillan titles can be ordered from our website, www.panmacmillan.com, or from your local bookshop and are also available by post from:

Bookpost, PO Box 29, Douglas, Isle of Man IM99 1BQ

Credit cards accepted. For details:
Telephone: 01624 677237
Fax: 01624 670923
Email: bookshop@enterprise.net
www.bookpost.co.uk

Free postage and packing in the United Kingdom